INCREDIBLE ROADS

Written by Kay Barnham
Illustrated by Aaron Cushley

Contents

OXFORD
UNIVERSITY PRESS

Words to look out for ...

alter *(verb)*

alters, altering, altered
To alter something is
to change it.

amend *(verb)*

amends, amending, amended
to change something in
order to improve it

conceal *(verb)*

conceals, concealing,
concealed
to hide something or keep
it secret

disadvantage *(noun)*
something that is unhelpful
or that causes a problem

ensure *(verb)*

ensures, ensuring, ensured
To ensure that something
happens is to make sure
of it.

exclude *(verb)*

excludes, excluding, excluded
To exclude something
is to leave it out.

methodical *(adjective)*
careful, logical or
well-organized

reinforce *(verb)*

reinforces, reinforcing,
reinforced
To reinforce something
is to strengthen it.

On the move

Imagine all the places that roads can take you to and the sights you might see on the way ...

You might travel through a town or the countryside. Perhaps you'll go over a mountain pass or across a **valley**. Maybe you'll go through a desert or even under the sea!

Roads take us to incredible places. Look closely and you'll discover that roads themselves are incredible, too!

the Atlantic Road in Norway

Long before proper roads, people used tracks.

track

Tracks are formed by people going the same route again ...

... and again. These tracks were formed by people going where they wanted.

The Ridgeway in England is one of the oldest human tracks in the world. It was once followed by **Stone Age** travellers. Now, it's popular with walkers and cyclists.

The invention of the wheel changed travel forever. Carts were invented to carry people and goods. Journeys became easier and faster.

However, cart wheels sank into the soft tracks and got stuck. Wheels roll best on hard surfaces. The solution was ... roads!

Stone roads were built around 4000 years ago in the country that is now called Iraq.

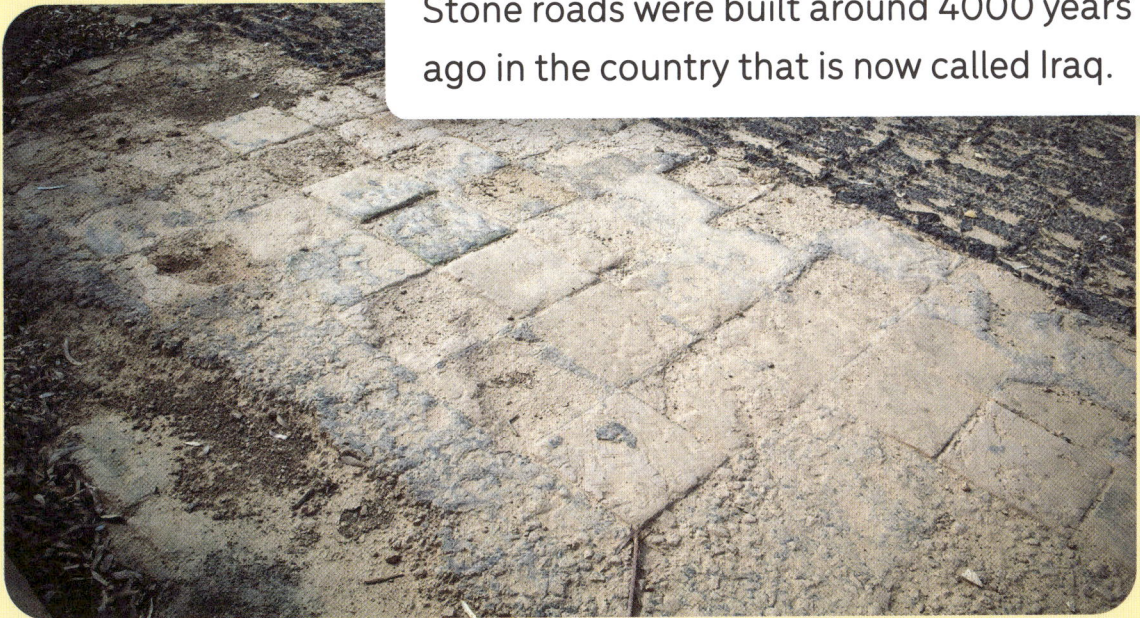

An early type of cart was called a chariot. Chariots rolled easily along stone roads.

chariot

Ancient Roman roads

More than 2000 years ago, the ancient Romans built roads that were smooth, **durable** and very straight. They were built so the Roman army could reach its destination as quickly as possible.

As their **empire** grew, so did its road network. Soon, 80 000 kilometres (km) of roads covered the Roman Empire. Many are still used today.

This road in Italy linked important Roman cities.

To build a road, the ancient Romans first cleared a route and marked it out using wooden posts or stones. They then dug a **trench** into the ground. This trench was filled with different layers of material: crushed rocks, small stones and pebbles, and then cement. Finally, large stone **slabs** were laid on top.

slabs

cement

small stones and pebbles

rocks

Road engineers still use methods like this today, though they use different materials.

Mountain roads

When the land changes, roads might need to be amended.

Some hills and mountains are so steep that cars can't drive straight up them. Engineers solve this problem by building roads that zigzag instead. The roads are longer as a result, but the slopes are gentler.

The Stelvio (say: *stel-vee-oh*) Pass in Italy has 48 sharp 'hairpin' bends. Some of its corners are so sharp, they are almost **U-turns**!

To amend something is to change it in order to improve it.

The Yungas (say: *yoon-gahs*) Road in Bolivia, South America, is a narrow mountain road that twists and turns through the Amazon rainforest. With no barriers and steep drops of over a kilometre, it is so dangerous that it's known as 'Death Road'.

In 2007, a new road was opened nearby. With fewer vehicles on the Yungas Road, the area is filling with wildlife.

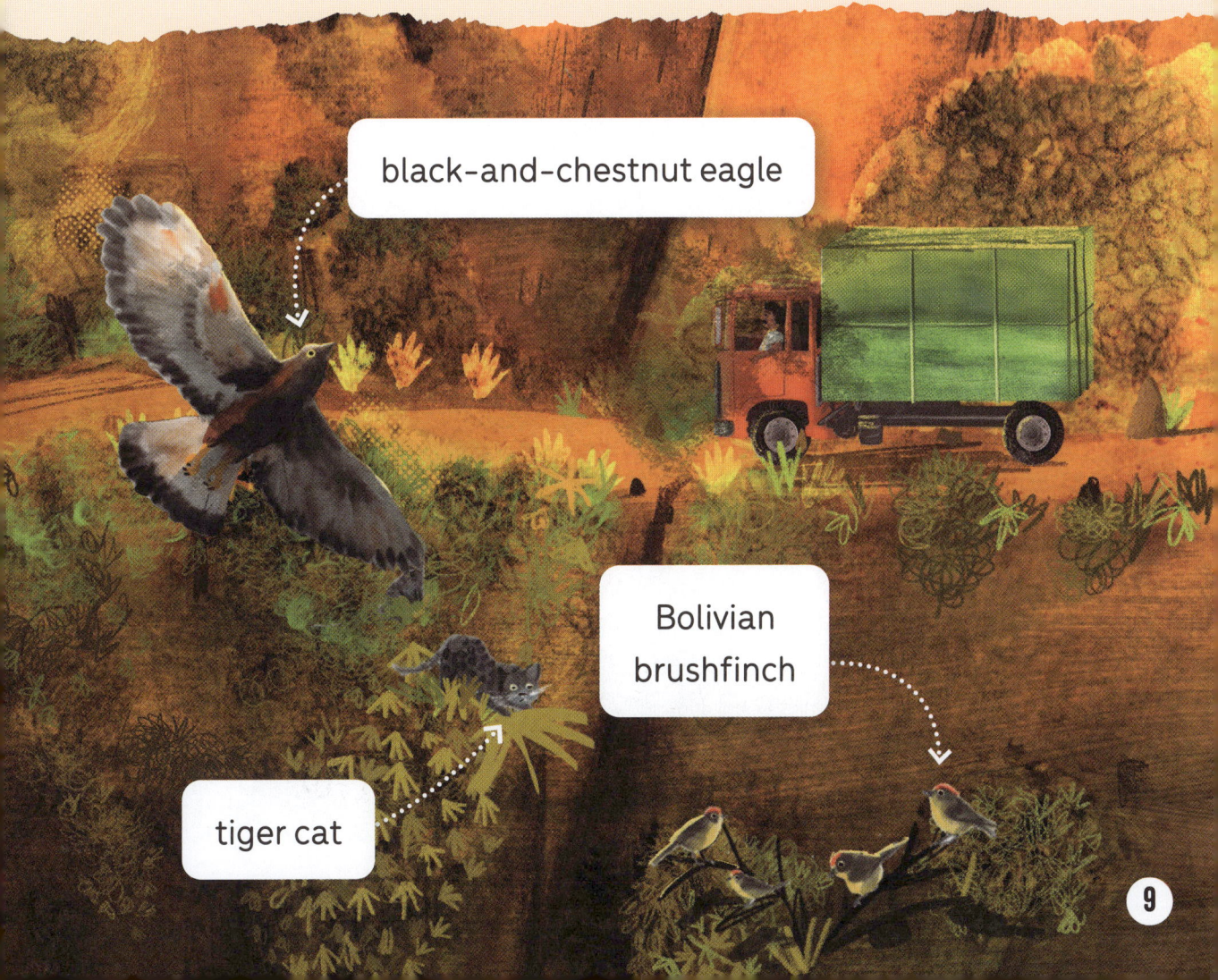

black-and-chestnut eagle

Bolivian brushfinch

tiger cat

Some places are very difficult to reach.

The village of Guoliang (say: *gwor-lee-ahng*) is perched high in the mountains in China. Until 1977, the only way to visit the village was by climbing hundreds of steep mountain steps. The villagers solved the problem by making a new road. They blasted a corridor through the cliff!

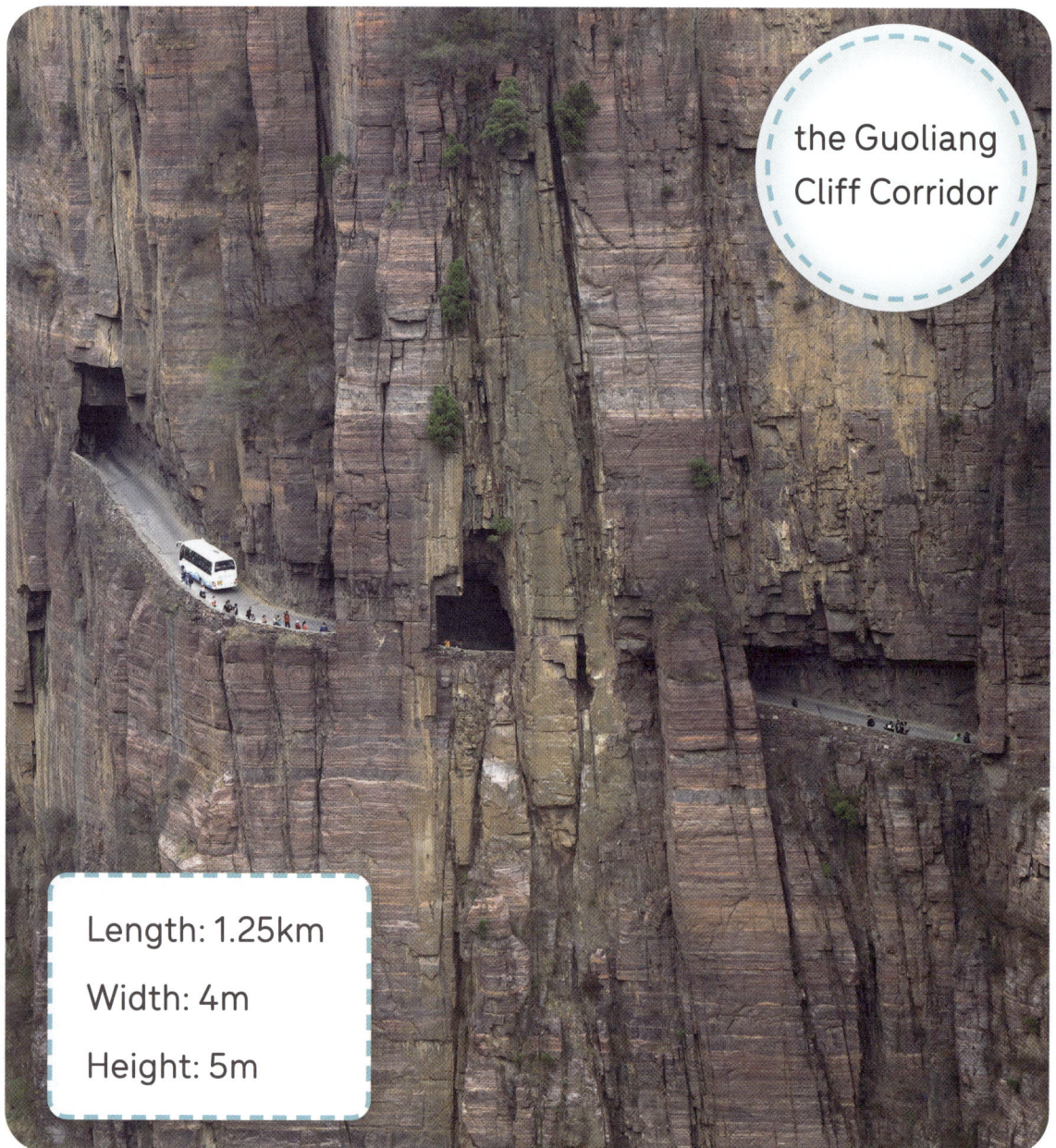

the Guoliang Cliff Corridor

Length: 1.25km

Width: 4m

Height: 5m

Coastal roads

Nearly half of the people in the world live within 50km of the coast. Coastal roads allow people to travel easily between the towns and cities where they live.

Chapman's Peak Drive in South Africa is carved into cliffs. It's important people drive carefully here. On one side, there are rock faces. On the other side, there's a steep drop to the sea below.

Coastal roads like Chapman's Peak Drive often have amazing views!

Roads on bridges

Bridges are great shortcuts! They can cut journey times. Some bridges are roads that pass over water, valleys and uneven ground. They connect places and people.

Bridges ensure that a journey is smooth, by carrying vehicles over obstacles.

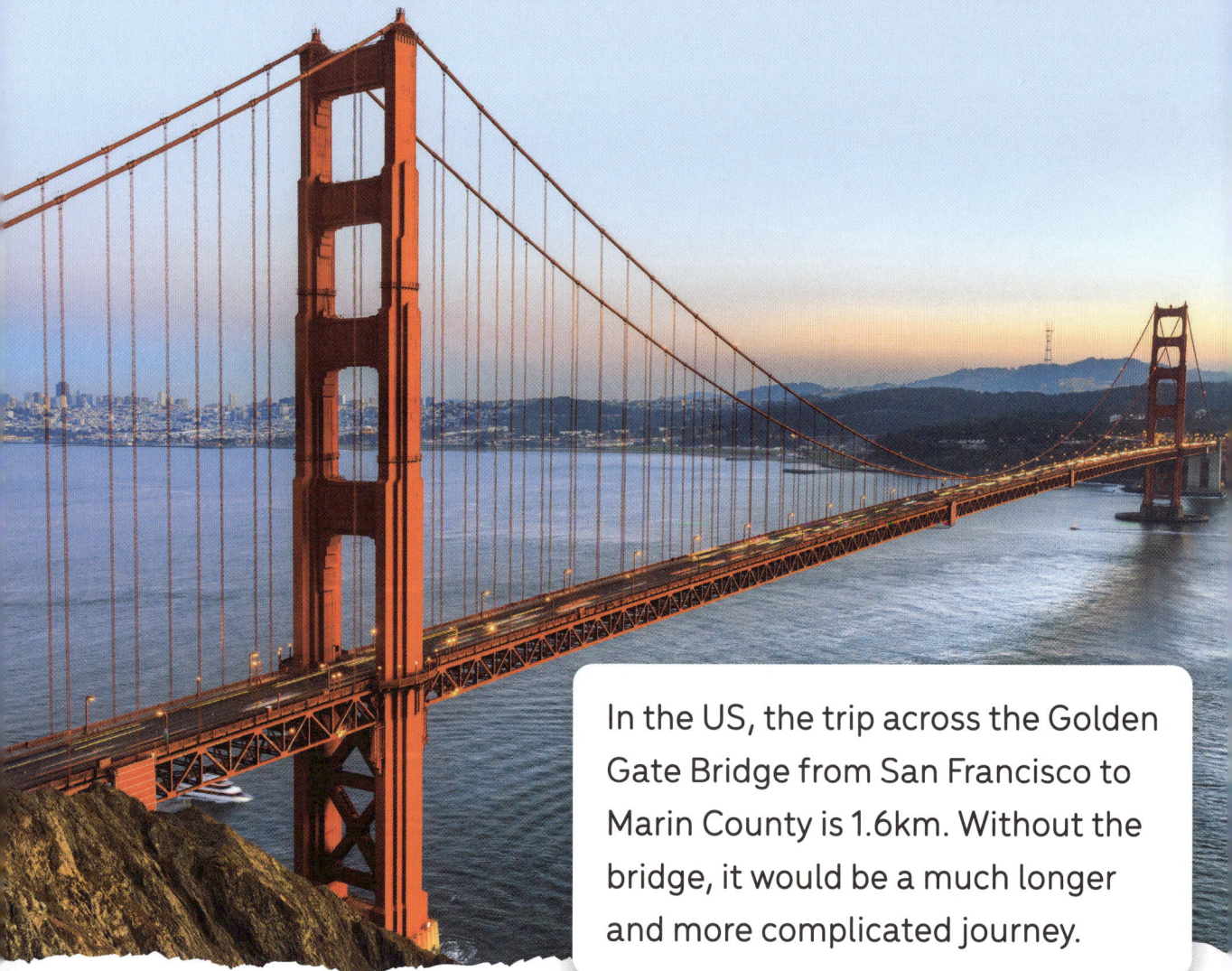

In the US, the trip across the Golden Gate Bridge from San Francisco to Marin County is 1.6km. Without the bridge, it would be a much longer and more complicated journey.

To ensure that something happens is to make sure of it.

Road junctions

Road **junctions** can allow drivers to leave or join large roads, like motorways. When motorways meet, things can become more complicated. Traffic may need to travel under or over another road to change direction.

These junctions allow traffic to move quickly and easily from one road to another.

Gravelly Hill in Birmingham, England, is known as the 'Spaghetti Junction' ... because it looks like spaghetti!

Road tunnels

If a mountain is too big to drive over, engineers may choose to build a road *through* it instead!

The Lærdal (say: *lehr-dal*) Tunnel connects the cities of Oslo and Bergen in Norway. It is 24.5km long, and is the longest road tunnel in the world. It goes under a big mountain and it takes 20 minutes to drive from one end to the other.

To keep drivers alert, there are enormous, brightly lit caves every 6km.

Undersea roads

Once, the only way to travel between the Faroe (say: *fair-oh*) Islands in the North Atlantic ocean was by boat. Undersea roads have changed everything!

The world's first undersea roundabout is beneath the Faroe Islands, near Scotland and Iceland.

Road tunnels are made using machines called tunnelling jumbos. Holes are drilled in the rock and filled with **dynamite**. Explosions blast away rock and the rubble is removed. The tunnel is then sprayed with concrete to reinforce it.

To reinforce something is to strengthen it.

The Øresun (say: *urr-eh-soond*) Bridge in Denmark includes underwater and overwater roads. Traffic travels over a bridge to a human-made island, where it disappears into a tunnel under the sea!

The tunnel was made from sections of concrete tube, laid in a trench along the bottom of the sea. Stone was placed on top to protect the new tunnel.

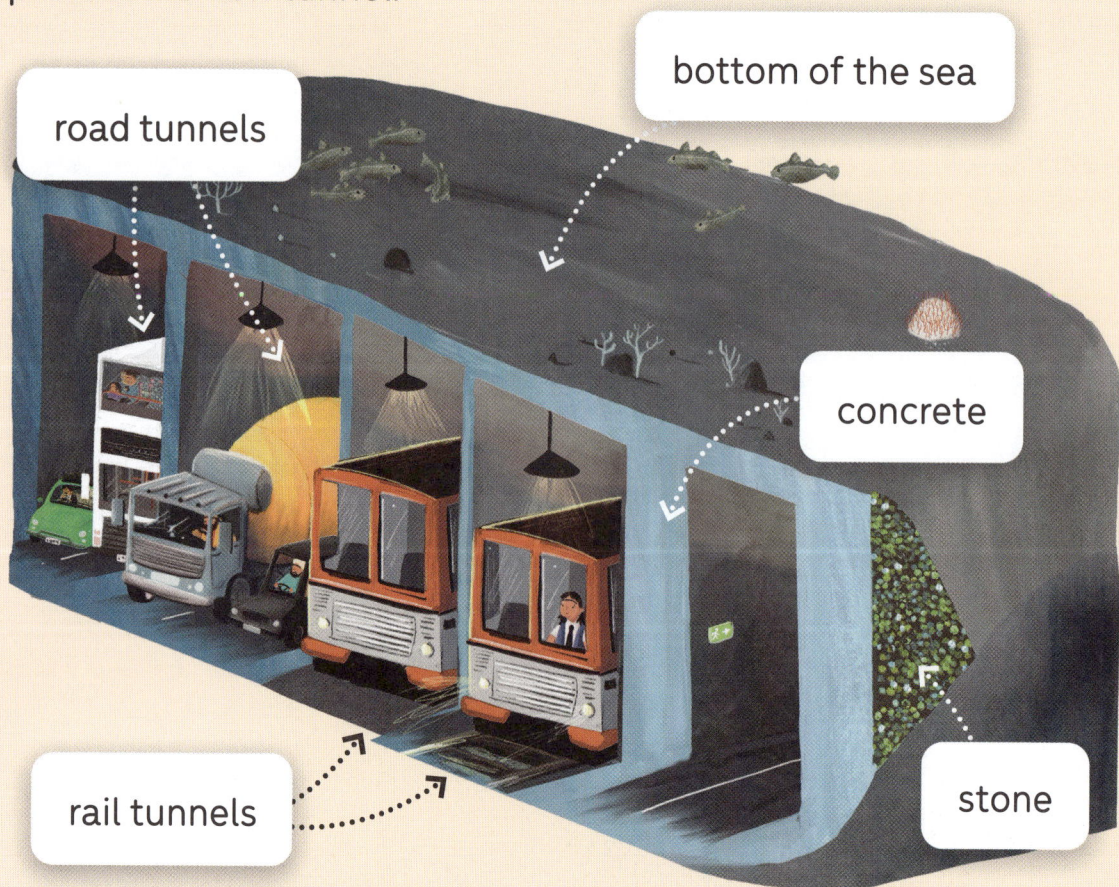

bottom of the sea

road tunnels

concrete

rail tunnels

stone

A causeway is a raised road that crosses water or low ground.

In France, the Passage du Gois (say: *pah-sahj-doo-gwah*) is a 4.2km causeway that links the main part of France with an island. For parts of the day and night, it is covered by water. When the tide goes out twice a day, the sea level falls and the causeway appears.

At high tide, the causeway is 4 metres (m) below the waves!

Ice roads

In parts of Canada, there are so many lakes that it's impossible to build a road that wiggles between them all. However, in the winter, everything changes. Lakes freeze solid, providing a stable base for the coolest roads in the world!

In spring, ice roads melt and vanish without a trace.

Engineers check the ice in a methodical way to make sure it is thick enough to carry traffic.

Methodical means careful, and logical or well-organized.

Desert roads

The Sahara Desert covers most of northern Africa. It took over 60 years to build a 4500km road across this baking hot desert. The road is called the Trans-Sahara Highway and it links northern Africa with Europe.

It's not just traffic that follows the Trans-Sahara Highway. Data travels along it, too! Cables are <u>concealed</u> under ground. These cables provide high-speed internet for millions of people.

To <u>conceal</u> something is to hide it or keep it secret.

Fast roads

Once a year, the roads of Monte-Carlo in Monaco are <u>altered</u> to become a racetrack! Roads are closed so the usual traffic vanishes. Instead, race cars roar around the circuit at speeds of over 300 kilometres per hour (kph).

Racing drivers travel round the circuit 78 times to complete the race.

It takes six weeks to transform Monaco into a race circuit ... and another three weeks to change it back again!

To <u>alter</u> something is to change it.

Airport roads

Some roads are used by aeroplanes, too!

A highway strip is a section of road that looks like a normal road, but it can also be used as a runway.

In Gibraltar, the airport's runway has a road running straight across it. People and cars had to stop whenever a plane landed or took off. In 2023, a tunnel under the runway was built ... but you can still cross over the road on foot!

Sponge roads

Roads bring some disadvantages. They take up space, can ruin wildlife habitats, and cause noise and pollution. When heavy rain washes **debris** (say: *deh-bree*) into drains, the drains can get blocked. This can lead to flooding.

Sponge roads are now being built in some places where flooding is a risk. Rain does not run off these roads, but soaks into them.

Sponge roads control flooding and recycle rainwater by using it to water trees and plants.

A disadvantage is something that is unhelpful or that causes a problem.

Roads of the future

Scientists have recently tested out roads with glow-in-the-dark markings. Roads soak up light during the day and then shine at night so people can see the road better.

In the future, we may have roads that fix themselves. **Solar** energy could be collected to power streetlights and signs. Cables under the road's surface might charge electric vehicles as they drive.

In the future, self-driving cars would <u>exclude</u> the need for drivers!

self-driving car

To <u>exclude</u> something is to leave it out.

Glossary

debris: remains of broken down things, like rocks or rubble

durable: able to withstand wear and pressure

dynamite: a powerful explosive

empire: a large group of places or countries ruled by a leader or government

engineers: people who design and build machines, roads and bridges

junctions: places where roads or railway lines join

runway: a long road which planes go down to increase their speed so they can take off

slabs: thick flat pieces of something

solar: to do with the sun or powered by the sun's energy

Stone Age: the period when humans used mainly stone for tools, before metalwork

trench: a long, narrow ditch or pit

U-turn: a turn to make a vehicle face the opposite direction

valley: a low area of land between hills or mountains

Index